CAIN
AND OTHER POEMS

WALTER KAUFMANN

CAIN
AND OTHER POEMS

*Enlarged edition,
including More Satirical Verse
A Light-hearted Guide to
Some Classics
and Taboo*

VINTAGE BOOKS
A Division of Random House / New York

AUTHOR'S NOTE

In recent weeks, Helen Bevington, Edward Cone, Keith Gunderson, Felix Kaufmann, and Alan Pearlman went over provisional versions of my manuscript and gave me encouragement and criticism that helped me greatly in making my final selections and revisions. I am also indebted to Timothy Seldes of Doubleday for his manifold kindness. And to Henry Hurwitz who, by accepting the "David" Cycle for *The Menorah Journal*, was the first to publish me.

W.K.
1962

FIRST VINTAGE BOOKS EDITION, APRIL 1971

Copyright © 1962, 1971 by Walter Kaufmann

All rights reserved under International and Pan-American Copyright Conventions. Published in the United States by Random House, Inc., New York. Distributed in Canada by Random House of Canada Limited, Toronto.
Originally published by Doubleday and Company, Inc., in 1962.

Library of Congress Catalog Card Number: 62-14131

Some of the poems in this book have appeared in the following publications to whom we give grateful thanks for permission to reprint: *Epitaph* in *Critique of Religion and Philosophy* by Walter Kaufmann, published by Harper & Row, Publishers, Incorporated, and Faber and Faber Ltd., Copyright © 1958 by Walter Kaufmann. *David: A Cycle* in *The Menorah Journal*, Copyright 1944 by Walter Kaufmann. *A Heretic's Sacraments* in *The American Scholar* and *Kaufmann's Laws* in *The Ladies' Home Journal*, Copyright © 1962 by The Curtis Publishing Company. *Desert-born god* in *Explorations: an annual on Jewish themes*, edited by Murray Mindlin with Chaim Bermant, Copyright © 1967 by The Institute of Contemporary History and Wiener Library. *The Fall: November 22, 1963* in *Of Poetry and Power: Poems Occasioned by the Presidency and by the Death of John F. Kennedy*, Copyright © 1964 by Basic Books, Inc. *Judgment, The Prince, Worms, Success Story* in *University: a Princeton Magazine*, in Winter 1963-64.

MANUFACTURED IN THE UNITED STATES OF AMERICA

FOR HAZEL

CONTENTS

BIBLE PORTRAITS (1961–62)

CAIN	21
THE FATHERS	22
Abraham	22
Isaac	24
Jacob	25
MOSES	26
SAUL	28
ELIJAH	30
HOSEA	32
JESUS	33
The Temptation	33
Gethsemane	34
The Crucifixion	35

A JOURNAL IN VERSE (1961)

AWAKENING	39
VITA NUOVA	40
WET ROAD	41
APRIL	42
WOUNDS	43
WHAT WEIGHS?	44
A RECORD	45
VIA MEDIA	46
DREAM	47
SPRING	48

SELF	49
PRETENSE	50
"DICHTEN"	51
REFLECTION	52
THEY READ	53
PEACE	54
ROMANTICISM	55
THE EICHMANN TRIAL	56
Witness	56
The Accused	58
To Israel	60
SELF-DECEPTION	61
DOGWOOD	62
CLIMBING	63
TREE LINE	64
A HERETIC'S SACRAMENTS	65
Baptism	65
Wedding	66
Death	67
SAINTS	68
THE CORE	69
TRAINS	70
SHORT POEMS	71
PROFESSIONALS	72
WHO CARES?	73
JUNE	74
FATHER FEENEY	75
SINS AGAINST THE SPIRIT	76
A FLOOD OF FRAGMENTS	77
KAUFMANN'S LAWS	78
TWO SENSES	79
PORTRAIT OF A LADY	80
PLAINTIVE SIGNALS	82

LIVING DANGEROUSLY	83
AIMLESS	84
SANCTION	86
COWARDICE TRIES TO REPEAT	87
IN THE DARK	88
EVERY REJECTION	89
DIARY	90
PACKAGED	91
ON TURNING FORTY	92
THEY	93
THE SENTENCE	94
RELIGION	95
JULY	100
SLOW SOLITUDE	101
YET	102
BIRD	103
WORDS ARE LIKE INSECTS	104
FOR D	105
TO A READER	106
LATE AUGUST	107
LEAP	108
LOVE LETTER TO A DAUGHTER	109
RIDE	110
GOETHE'S CRITICS	111
A MIND AGAINST MADNESS	112
UNSHELTERED	113
AN INVOCATION	114
MY GOD	115
FOG	116
HOW FAR IS FAR?	117
SIR	118
DÉJÀ VU	119
AUTUMN	120

LOVE	121
AMOS' IMMORTAL COW	122
CHURCH SUPPER	123
RIDDLE	124
HOW MANY HOURS?	125
THE BURNING BUSH	126

INTERLUDE: TEN GERMAN POEMS
(1939–42)

YELLOWSTONE	135
KRIEGSAUSBRUCH, 1939	136
KEIN GOTT	137
STIMMEN	139
ALLMÄCHTGER GOTT	140
STERNENSCHICKSAL	142
EPITAPH	143
MARIA	144
SONNENUNTERGANG	145
REGEN	147

REMBRANDT AND OTHER POEMS
(1940–60)

EXILE (1940)	151
A WOMAN'S LOVE SONG	152
KABIR	153
HEART BEAT	154
THE CONDUCTOR	155
REMBRANDT	156
OCCUPATION	157

THE LEPER	158
THE CURTAIN	159
OLD LETTERS	160
HOW DOES ONE GROW?	161
THE OPENED HEART	162
NIETZSCHE	163
DO NOT PRAY	165
GOD	166
IN HEINE'S TRACES	167
NOVEMBER	168

MORE SATIRICAL VERSE (1947-69)

SOMEBODY ELSE'S GRASS	171
THE MODERN HOUSE	172
READING *The Unsilent Generation*	173
TEENAGER	174
LO-KU	175
SOCIOLOGIST'S LOVE SONG	175
DIALOGUE	175
WHEN	175
ANOTHER RIDDLE	176
THEODICY	177
DOUBTS ABOUT FREUD	178
A CROWD OF THOUSANDS	179
THE ACADEMIC ZOO	180

A LIGHT-HEARTED GUIDE TO SOME CLASSICS (1961)

ANTIGONE	183
TANTALUS' TRIBE	185

TABOO (1962-69)

THE TABOOBOO SONG	191
JUDGMENT	194
THE PRINCE	195
WORMS	196
DESERT-BORN GOD	197
SUCCESS STORY	198
DREAMS	199
FOX	200
THE FALL	201
PEACE	204
FOLIAGE	205
ELM	206

DAVID: A CYCLE (1943)

ABIGAIL	209
A HYMN OF JOY	210
A PRAYER OF DAVID	211
SAUL AMONG THE PROPHETS	212
THE DEATH OF SAUL	215
KING DAVID'S DANCE	216
DAVID AND BATHSHEBA	218
BATHSHEBA	218
DAVID	220
BATHSHEBA	223
ABSALOM'S DEATH	226
THE LAST PSALM OF DAVID	227
ABISHAG	228

BIBLE PORTRAITS

(1961–62)

CAIN

To break the sleepless pain that Abel's placid,
insensitively peaceful face engendered
in his divinely discontented mind;
to purge his dreams of blood, his thoughts of acid,
and feel the world again; he had surrendered
to his surviving passion, raised his hand,

and struck—releasing feelings he was first
to sense and savor and not to endure.
He saw his brother bleeding like the sheep
Abel had slaughtered without qualm or care;
peace fled as terror crowned his frightening sleep
and eyes, no longer placid, thundered: Cursed

art thou to live forever without peace!—
Adam and Eve, his wife, his children died
before he learned to pitch his tent in time,
and when the waters rose and did not cease,
drowning, he rued his envy and his crime,
and cursed his hand that had not known to write.

THE FATHERS

ABRAHAM

I

Awakened by his name, old Abraham,
roused from a nightmare that at once had fled,
replied, his eyes still sightless, Here I am,
and was all readiness and nameless dread.

For three days he spoke little and saw less,
doing as in a sleep what he was bidden,
prepared to do what he could not express,
while he that had commanded him had hidden.

But from that second sleep he also woke,
hearing his name again, and Here I am
brought back the nightmare, and his blindness broke,
and in the thicket he beheld a ram.

II

What did he think of those three days as he
returned, his sight restored, and saw the glance
his son, as from an ambush, furtively
shot at his bloody hands? Did not the trance

that had protected him like night's black curtain
seem a lost haven now, compared to this
silent abandonment to the uncertain?
To hear and not to see is faith and bliss—

but now the unrecorded trial came,
when Sarah drowned in wordless apathy,
and no voice helped, and no one called his name:
he had no task but was condemned to see.

ISAAC

When age had dulled his sight, Rebecca grew
more distant and his smaller son reminded
him of a childhood dream. The world withdrew,
and words rushed in as his old eyes were blinded.

While Esau's deeper voice and talk of deer
distracted him, the high-pitched, plaintive sound
of Jacob's filled him with forgotten fear
as if it were his own and he were bound.

He had been blessed though Ishmael was first,
and felt this blessing was a thing to shun:
it smelled of sacrifice; but if reversed . . .
He planned, in vain, to bless his first-born son.

JACOB

When dark had sealed his solitude, and dawn
was likely to bring death, he did not say,
Remove this cup, but let thy will be done!
He wrestled God until the sky grew grey,

and when God saw that He could not prevail
and wounded him and pleaded, Let me go!
a weary man that once was small and frail
mastered his terror and forgot his awe

and, seeing God, said, I will not unless—
my father said, my blood, my flesh and bone,
Jacob no more but Israel—you bless
me that have fought and conquered God, alone.

MOSES

Not valleys, lakes, and gentle hills—
a man of mountains: when he sees
his brother scourged, he burns, and kills
the wielder of the whip, and flees

into a land of sand and rock
where courage counts, not faith or hope,
becomes a shepherd, leads his flock
up on a savage mountain slope,

and in a wilderness of stone
finds strength that feeds upon what burns,
and grows, and kindles flames. Alone,
he leaves his exile and returns

to light a fire that no scourge
consumes, a blaze whips only fan,
leads hence his people, and to purge
the dross and make the slave a man,

he drives his wretched herd into
the desert to behold what he
had seen—people who never knew
mountains, lightning, or liberty.

Days without water, hungry weeks:
what he had lit was soon consumed.
He learned the patience of the peaks,
and dying branches he relumed.

There was no trail, the climb was steep,
no man had thrilled to what he saw—
and on a flock of bleating sheep
a lonely man imposed a law,

moulding the mountain's thunderous voice
into a monumental word,
and challenged them to make a choice
that humanized a servile herd.

Where only crags stood out from sand
and life was will and not delight,
he taught them till in any land
their souls would seek the unreached height.

When only two of those he led
from slavery survived, and all
the others had been born and bred
under the challenge of his call—

triumphant past imaginings,
he blessed them, and soared out of sight,
sailing on undiminished wings,
and died, an eagle in his flight.

SAUL

The twilight of his doubt endured, and froze
Agag of Amalek, the haughty snake,
writhing in blood-soaked fetters as
the ancient Samuel, too old to judge,
still clasps in cruel hands, that shake
with age, a broadsword he wields like a sledge,
    and hews the captive king to pieces—still
    the doubter hears the old man's voice: "the Lord
    rejects you, Saul, because you did not kill
    Agag of Amalek as you were told."

Awed by the man's inhuman certainty,
Saul had cried out: "Forgive me, and relent!"
Too old to judge, and trembling, he
had roared back: "Do you think God is a man
who rues his word? The Lord does not repent,
and will complete what he began.
    He wants obedience, not burnt offerings,
    and has forsaken you, rebellious Saul."
    His doubt endured: If even human kings
    could rise to mercy, could God be so small?

And if the Lord repented that he made
me king of Israel, why could he not
rue his rejection? And was he that bade
me kill Agag of Amalek
and, like a beast, destroyed him, sent by God
or a false voice, and was I weak
    to let his word freeze me in solitude?
    God's voice is not so clear and sharp.
    Twilight and weakness grow, I sit and brood.
    For God's sake, send for David and his harp!

ELIJAH

I

"Years of unbroken skies and sands,
the era of the boneless crowds
that have antennae but no hands,
that live in dust and know no clouds,

were finished in one flash when I
taunted their hollow faith and feasts,
brought down white fire from the sky,
and slew four hundred fifty priests.

The land is green again, the drought
faded into a boastful tale,
no idol left, but though they shout
to God again their hearts mean Baal.

The desert I inherited:
for forty nights I walked till I
saw where a sky of burning lead
is broken by Mount Sinai;

for forty days, sand, wind, and sun,
no human voice, no human face,
and then this cleft—perhaps the one
where Moses hid from unseen grace.

But he lived in a man-sized age,
broke granite tablets, and prevailed;
mine is the day of priest and sage
and paltriness, and I have failed.

I, only I am left; and yet
I have not come here to despair:
I seek the voice of Moses; let
the jaundiced Jezebel beware!"

II

A tempest struck the crags and tore
black bolders from the rocky spires,
an earthquake split the mountain's core,
releasing serpent-bodied fires—

to man-sized men, winged seraphim
attending God's own blazing voice—
mere fire, quake, and wind to him,
nothing of God. He veiled his face

when silence fell like night, and found
his call inside his mind, at first
a whisper almost lacking sound;
but then it grew, and when it burst

like lightning from his darkness he
saw Hazael and Jehu whom
he must anoint: who bent a knee
to Baal their ruthless wars consume;

his mantle falls; Elisha slays
Baal's minions who escaped the sword;
Elijah rides—he could not raise
his people—lonely to the Lord.

HOSEA

What do those preachers know of love who claim
that once a doubt thrusts through your staggered mind
and kills the sleeping guards of faith, the game
is over? Curtain gone, no longer blind,
    love can no longer hide, the stage is bare,
    the play begins. He went and wed a whore,

buried his soul in her, but not his eyes,
and let her treachery become his world.
She fed him wanton but translucent lies,
betrayed him under oaks and in the field,
    but was no worse than ingrate Israel;
    and more and more he felt what God must feel,

whose love outlasts not only doubt but fact
repeated thousandfold, though neither slumber
nor velvet-pawed oblivion can distract
his cruel heart: sins that no man could number
    he that smites Job and crushes some who rue
    forgives to some who do know what they do.

JESUS

THE TEMPTATION

He, too, like Moses and Elijah, dwelt
for forty days in desert solitude;
yet God did not appear to him: he felt
the presence of the devil's voice that said,
"Behold these stones: speak and they shall be bread!"
replied, "Man does not live by bread alone"—
but soon turned water into wine.

He saw himself stand on a pinnacle:
"Cast yourself down," the devil seemed to prod,
"angels will save you." To the voice from hell
Jesus replied, "You shall not tempt your God"—
but soon vied with Elisha's feats and awed
a crowd by raising Jairus' dead daughter,
withered a tree, and walked on water.

The devil promised Jesus world-wide fame
and glory that no pharaoh or king
or prophet ever equalled: yea, his name
would be like God's, and men would worship him,
if he would bow to Satan's stratagem.
He answered, "Worship none except the Lord"—
but Satan's promise was fulfilled.

GETHSEMANE

How did they know what he had said
in prayer while they slept?
Between their dreams they saw his dread,
his pallor and his sweat.

He did not want to be alone
and feared that he might fail.
Friendless, Elijah faced the throne
and scores of priests of Baal.

But Jesus wanted company,
was wretched and afraid:
he was like you, he was like me,
and yet he was true God.

And you and I, small and despairing,
shall gain salvation's wreath,
while men who matched Elijah's daring
shall howl and gnash their teeth.

O Jesus, come and cleanse the den
of sanctimonious beasts:
leave us Elijah and such men,
and you can have the priests!

THE CRUCIFIXION

The veil of the temple was torn, they say,
the earth did quake, and the rocks were rent,
the graves were opened, the dead rose that day—
and after waiting three days they went

into the city, appearing to many.
The earth quakes for those who suffer the loss,
but the dead remain dead, and I doubt that any
were raised. What was raised was only the cross,

which towered above the tortured Jew
and kept on growing, and grew above
his tales and his teaching until it threw
a shadow over the children of

his parents, his people, a shadow lined
with edges of scarlet that spread like diseases,
infecting the heathens' barbarian mind.
The graves were opened—for the people of Jesus.

A JOURNAL IN VERSE

(1961)

AWAKENING

Stark as a dream, not softened by
a conscious hope, yet a reply
to a pervasive longing—I
was, till now unaware.

A flash, a vision, an encounter—
dams are broken that my cowardice
had built, a rush of power,
no escape.

A word, a woman, or a page—
each time the dread as torrents rage
toward a ravine, light floods the stage,
I plunge awake.

VITA NUOVA

Near-night was welcome when
the buried talent burst
out of the grave dusk, like
a second sun. Again
there was a future, thirst,
and life.

The full moon's light is not
like day, brisk, hard, and hot;
what lies ahead is slow
and cool, almost as sweet
as dark had seemed; but now
I'll die complete.

WET ROAD

Red lights drive fiery beams
through rain and stone
into the depth of dreams:
nothing is prone,
and gaudy flames descend
to darkness without end.

APRIL

Budding twigs sway
in the wind out there;
inside all is grey,
weary, and bare.

Rocking, they dream
of the spring to come;
rain makes them gleam,
not, like me, numb.

They will burst open,
unfold, and glow;
I, without hoping,
will still work in the snow.

WOUNDS

Mind's wounds close not.
Like leaves, thoughts hover,
drift down, and cover
old thoughts that rot.

New thoughts don't matter:
blow, and they scatter
like bees from a hive.
Mind's wounds survive.

Days are like snow,
heavy and glare,
endless nights bare
hell's flames below.

WHAT WEIGHS?

What weighs still
like Oedipus' crime
crushing the mind?
Common men kill,
no one has time,
all men are blind.

Murder of kings
has become news
—"kill autocrat"—
Job's sufferings,
Odysseus' woes,
not even that.

Clytemnestra's ax
calls for a gloss
because it seems odd.
Auschwitz' smokestacks
dwarf one Jew on the cross
and the death of God.

A RECORD

A record, a rocket,
date upon date,
three books in one pocket:
what still has weight?

A record, a rocket,
doubt upon doubt,
ten crimes in one docket:
what still stands out?

Datum on datum,
hit upon hit,
a man is an atom,
atoms are split.

VIA MEDIA

Silence torments
and is yet sweet,
while confidence
begets deceit
and vents
the pressure past endurance that
descends where thoughts don't dare to dwell.

Heaven is talk and trust
and lies:
how could tongue tell
what breaks mind's girth?

Silence, a thrust
toward hell,
but wise.

And art is earth.

DREAM

To write granite verse and prose
polished hard simple and
dazzling as a sphinx with a broken nose
in endless sand.

No passing image of what
is no matter
but a presence time can not
shatter.

SPRING

Mirrored lights dancing down the street
in a bubbling river
greet
blossoms that shiver
on shining trees.

SELF

"I've always said," they say;
"that's how I am," and "you know me."
I do indeed: a stone by day.
But I? A cloud. I cannot see
what even now I seemed to be.
What I have said, I may
have been once; it is not
my present nature. What
am I to be or say?
I am the potter and the clay.

PRETENSE

Like air, men need the slippery skin
of blind pretense to love, respect,
and worship what their intellect
would punish with a graceless grin.

Inconstant is man's speckled heart,
a mask of slime
that changes contours; for a time
a pose congeals,
one plays a part
and says one feels.

To live without a skin
like things!
To be a violin
and have no strings!

The slippery darkness of the heart
is broken by the moon
of mind,
and puppets that before her rise
had gone through motions, being blind,
can act their roles with open eyes
like instruments
that call the tune.
Pretense
that knows itself is art.

"DICHTEN"

Nights of thoughts condense
into an image so
simple sublime and intense
that no diorite pharaoh
has more eloquence.

REFLECTION

Glaring bulbs that hurt,
vulgar and shocking
colors that scream

muddy waters convert
to a gently rocking
indefinite dream.

THEY READ

They read
as they drink:
not to think.

They read
as they feed:
not to retain—

as one takes a pill
to kill
pain.

PEACE

Lights on the ceiling
in the usual places.
No more feeling.
Thoughts, worn threadbare,
no longer dare
show their faces.

What used to drill
through my mind all night,
I recall at will,
without feeling,
like the light
on the ceiling.

Retraced slowly,
groove after groove:
piercing ache.
Seen all at once, wholly,
it fails to move.
I care not if I wake.

ROMANTICISM

I heard an old harlot sighing:
Look at the green trees and the dew!
I heard a young whore replying:
What are the green trees to you?

I can see how a poet thrills
to the arias of nightingales
and to valleys of daffodils;
but when he faints and fails

or, worse, has intimations
and fills with ecstasy
pages of ostentations,
what is all that to me?

I doubt that a human heart
could ever have felt half the rapture
that reams of romantic art
never entirely capture.

I heard a young whore sighing:
Some of them felt all they said.
I heard an old harlot replying:
They strain, but their hearts are dead.

THE EICHMANN TRIAL

WITNESS

Mommie, why did you make me wear
my Sabbath dress when it is not
a holiday? The field is bare,
and we are going to be shot.

Mommie, why do the women whine?
Mommie, this is no holiday.
Mommie, why do we stand in line?
Why don't we try to run away?

A woman tried to run; they caught her.
A soldier: Whom shall I shoot first?
I had no words. They took my daughter.
One yanked my hair. I heard the burst.

I could not breathe, deep in the pit,
so many corpses over me.
I clawed my way. Somebody bit
my arm, somebody grabbed my knee.

I clawed my way into the air,
I saw the light, the light felt good;
I looked around, no one was there.
I walked away and reached the wood.

When I woke up I was alone,
my parents, child, and sister dead.
I banged my head against a stone,
against a stone I banged my head.

The pit was covered with fresh dirt.
I clawed and dug. What was my sin?
Why was I spared? My fingers hurt.
I want to climb back in! Back in!

THE ACCUSED

He looks like a mouse, not like a great cat;
he is thoroughly unromantic.
He is proud that he was a bureaucrat,
and he is still pedantic.

Why can't a monster be big and black?
Some like administration,
and what creates hell is sometimes a lack
of feeling and imagination.

"I was a small sausage, not one of the great,
nor especially bad or good.
I did what I did without any hate;
I merely did what I could.

I did not ask for evidence
but for authorization,
and my blind trust gave me a sense
of fulfillment and gratification.

I am a man without any bias,
and I did not deceive or defraud.
My Christian upbringing was very pious,
and I still believe in God.

I did not allow my thoughts to dwell
on the awful things I had seen.
I did my work, and I did it well,
and most of it was routine.

I never could have slept had I
remembered what I knew.
Of course, I sent them all to die,
but I never killed one Jew."

TO ISRAEL

You want to be like other nations still
and feel, like Shylock, that if we resemble
the others in the rest, why not in this
insistence on the justice of the Gentiles?

About a guilt as plain as any ever
you rant and argue, strain to add some stones
to Everest, and wish to seal the crime
by spilling blood, though it cries out like Cain's.

Are not three thousand years sufficient time
to rise above the lust to ape the nations
and do the prophets' bidding, changing spears
to pruning hooks and, with an equal daring,
make justice break her sword, and once again
become a light in darkness to the world?

SELF-DECEPTION

Like one who dares not ask and tries
to keep her mind from thinking lest
an inquiry reveal if pressed
that love is lost and her faith lies

is one who hopes despite all signs
of cosmic infidelities
discounting what his reason sees
for comfort found in dreamed designs.

DOGWOOD

Dogwood pagodas, serene without weight,
wise as old poets, fresh and sweet
as young women in pink and white.

CLIMBING

Over the brilliant branches of
twisted dead trees,
beyond outclimbed love
and forgotten paths, one sees,
almost lost in the deep,
what prompted hope and despair;
and the final ascent, sunny and steep,
is a dazzling dare.

TREE LINE

Groves of pines
clinging to rocks
dead roots anchored
in windswept cracks
fingers and arms
raised toward the sky
gestures of protest
a visual cry
frozen courage
windswept and light
happy to suffer
death at a height.

A HERETIC'S SACRAMENTS

BAPTISM

We chose a name, knowing that you, not we,
must bear its burden, and we recognize
this symbol of responsibility
almost too great for us. We are not wise—

hence you exist—and we shall fail while prone
to feel you failed. May you some day forgive
your parents, and we hope when you are grown
you will sometimes be happy that you live.

WEDDING

Grateful and joyous love discerns
all that is best, all, all
that calls for hope.

Wounded, an animal, it turns
and turns round what is small,
and has to grope,

deprived of sight, for what is strong,
and, sleepless, cannot dream.
In agony

it charges, counts, and recounts wrong;
and features, once loved, scream
for charity.

Knowing all this, I wed thee: wound
my soul, be thou my rack,
let us unite.

Love is not love that dies when pruned:
cut deep, true love grows back
to greater height.

DEATH

When I am dead do not play dolls and dress
my body in a suit before you lay
it in a box to sleep! Should I sleep less
if you disposed of me some other way?

Drown, burn, or bury me; forget
sometimes; but when you do remember me
recall us as we were, without regret,
and honor our love with honesty.

SAINTS

Born to perdition are most men indeed
regardless of what they do,
as if St. Augustine's merciless creed
and St. Thomas' and Calvin's were true.

Hunger, disease, and hopelessness swell
human devils' caprice.
But when men die they escape from this hell
into eternal peace.

Saints, seeing other men wronged worse than Job,
do not challenge God to his face,
but imagine worse sufferings inside the earth's globe,
and praise God's grace.

THE CORE

I

What is hard
to follow
often hides lard
or is hollow.

II

The age of the onion
thought and feeling run thin
the time of technique
the age of the skin.

Lack of a core
one tries to conceal
writers contrive
and critics peel

skins without end
and reach no heart
call it philosophy
writing and art.

TRAINS

Waiting for sleep. The voice
of a distant train. I once made,
far away, a choice.
Have I finally paid?

Trains since childhood, without
me and with me, puncture the night.
Always there is the doubt,
did I do right?

SHORT POEMS

Flowing garments of ample plot,
paint's mute mystery may protect
skinny feelings and flabby thought;

music's mellifluent dialect
or the expanse of undisciplined size
may evoke uncomprehending respect,

pleasing dumb ears or defeating worn eyes,
hiding what short verse would quickly reveal:
swamps that are garnished with fireflies.

Poets denature the word to conceal
lack of meaning and strength to exclude,
impotent lust to think and feel.

Poems like statues—unadorned, nude,
terse as a torso and yet complete,
fusing some thoughts, some tropes, and a mood—

venture a mind beyond retreat.

PROFESSIONALS

We are professionals, we have no room
for a Plato, Spinoza, or Hume,
who covers the world in one book;
what we like is a good hard look
at a single diminutive topic,
    a teacher, a talker, a scholar,
    a colleague without any choler,
and an eye that is microscopic.

We write papers for scholarly journals,
so solid they have no kernels;
our arguments always look tight,
and though we don't know how to write,
there are always footnotes and rows
of symbols to break up our prose.

Solid, circumscribed, and
showing a thorough command
of all the most recent papers,
we may not be movers and shapers;
but if one is only solid,
    a teacher, a talker, a scholar,
    a colleague without any choler,
one has a right to be pallid.

WHO CARES?

In city nights fitfully lit
by a chaos of vanishing cars
blaring frantic fragments of hits
of the week sung by vanishing stars

we must choose. Who cares for our fate?
A few nights and one disappears.
Yet our choices gain weight
as they grow in the mind through the years.

JUNE

Still dampness after unrefreshing rain,
no sun, no breeze, no distinct clouds, no air,
a lasting, suffocating pain
that numbs the mind and kills the will to care.

And what spawned the uncaring brutes who shot
dumb children and developed the fine art
of genocide and cross, if not
this sticky torpor—quicksand of the heart?

FATHER FEENEY

Outside the Church is no salvation.
With acrobatic exegesis
the Church attenuates this thesis:
non-Catholics can escape damnation.

Said Feeney: You have to belong
to Mother Church or go to hell.
Said Mother Church: You infidel;
keep quiet, Feeney, you are wrong.

The Father claimed his view was true
and backed up by one pope at least;
his archbishop defrocked the priest,
the Jesuits expelled him too.

Then he received an invitation
to come and clear himself in Rome.
It's forged, he said, and stayed at home.
The answer: excommunication.

Now even Feeney ought to know,
if he is right then he is wrong,
for he himself does not belong:
where does he think that he will go?

SINS AGAINST THE SPIRIT

A large body of work that lacks all wit,
thoughts that don't breathe but are content to sit,
wrapped up in darkness—a retired mole
who is too old to dig—a musty soul
that has no windows, only storage space—
a dead mind buried in a loamy face.
Pretentious verbiage that does not make sense
to the bare eye; examined through a lens,
a tissue of diseases, an offense
against wit, candor, and intelligence.

A FLOOD OF FRAGMENTS

A flood of fragments foams
into my weary night
grammar has ebbed away
in the black undertow
the iridescent shells
of thought
and broken feelings
driftwood
would drift
would sleep
become a fragment
foam
dissolve
in
darkness

KAUFMANN'S LAWS

This is the first of Kaufmann's Laws:
the weakling always fails because
somebody else did wrong.
The second: those who don't despair
but grow when others are unfair
give proof that they are strong.

TWO SENSES

Children, when I was a child,
would be told: be seen, not heard.
For the ear, not for the eye
is the public speaker's word.
Poems, to show what they mean,
must be heard as well as seen.

PORTRAIT OF A LADY

Interrogation Center in Germany, 1945

I

With bleakly pleading eyes she talked
of a far winter when the rivers froze:
caught by the Germans, she had walked
from wall to wall when it was death to doze,
and could have warmth and food and bed
if she would only tell them what she knew—
and told, and saw men hanged till dead—
and she was raped—but if I were inclined,
that would be different and she would not mind:
who else could help her now but I?
She has no mind but does not want to die.

II

In every cell they tell the same,
as children spell, scared without shame,
and give no picture, dwelling on the frame.
They tell it well, and they are not to blame,
for hell
is not a lake of flame.

III

Was there no time for death? Were they too busy
selling their bodies to the butchers? Why

did she walk back and forth till she was dizzy
and starve and kill if there was time to die?
Was it to tell it now to strangers,
barely listening as they measure
the pleasure
of her breasts against the dangers?

IV

To put down
one stroke that finishes a bold design,
some die content. In hell
she dreaded death. Her body all she has to give,
the burnt-out shell
still craves to live.

V

Outside the spring is pretty,
and the women are nicer outside;
for her likes they have no pity,
and they have a lot more pride.
But when the river was frozen,
how many of them would have chosen
torture or suicide?
Outside are flowering trees,
and outside people look well.
Inside the rivers still freeze,
inside is the void of hell.

PLAINTIVE SIGNALS

Plaintive signals, speeding sirens
raised me from the dead of sleep.
What I dared not ask you waking
you had answered in my dream.

Rooms that someone loved in ruins
you abandoned and alone
smiling while your mind is aching
dreaming as the sirens scream.

Admiration charred by knowledge
in a sudden deadly light
mansions where the heart dwelt breaking
and the ashes barely gleam.

LIVING DANGEROUSLY

Whence should I take the strength as the breakers that raise
    me,
foaming with joy as they laugh at my merry defiance,
crush and submerge me and grind me, as soon as I tire,
into the sand and sharp stones and the broken shells that,
when they were whole in the light, were so brilliant to look
    at?

How I enjoy being whirled in the undertow when I
still have the strength to fight with the breakers that bruise
    me!
But in the life that I have elected one cannot
rest like those gathering dust in the sand's sheltered dryness.

Unprotected by anything save my own effort,
I taste the naked encounter with forces that others
worship and dream of in shells while insisting that they are
guardians of mysteries that in the realm of the broken
shells are no longer so distant, but beauty and danger:

beauty as long as one lacks not the power to fight them,
utter despair as soon as weariness weakens
that oceanic resistance to fate without which
dangerous living and daring is hopeless dejection.

AIMLESS

Aimless
she wandered
through a maze
of nameless
streets
and squandered
her endless days

defeats
had drowned
her will

at the sound
of the chimes
on the hill
she would
sometimes
enter
a store
and stare
as if
she suddenly understood

her despair
had no core
no center
but was complete
without a goal

sometimes stiff
and brittle
that she might break
sometimes sharp
then a little
dim
like a lonely lake
because
she could not swim
then she was
an Aeolian harp
in a gale

always
it was whole
and filled her days.

SANCTION

To care, to paint, to write, to do
something that might endure above
the daily dust, to go beyond
quaint feelings to abiding love,

nothing constrains us: force and God
can constitute sublime duress,
no reason makes responsible,
nothing obliges but noblesse.

COWARDICE TRIES TO REPEAT

Cowardice tries to repeat
  throws that succeed,
seeks what is obsolete,
  snug as a creed,
lacking the courage to meet
  unheard-of need.

Simply by being the first,
  undefiled flings,
those that are unrehearsed
  are granted wings.
What is repeated is cursed:
  rote never sings.

IN THE DARK

In the dark the floor lamp glistens,
edged in gold by distant splendor
like a granite lotus pillar.
In the darkness no one listens,
wounded hearts cannot surrender,
and the night grows ever stiller.

Softly falling, listless rain,
hopeless, gentle, and persistent,
cannot save the dying elm.
Language fails when faced with pain,
jealousy makes deaf and distant,
words cannot invade its realm.

Who turned stone into the sphinx?
will, into a sculpted face?
lovely lotus, into granite?
Grief, denied expression, thinks
how it might burst into space
like a new-born planet.

EVERY REJECTION

Every rejection drives,
couched and plated and shined,
dime-store pearl-studded knives
into the diffident mind.

Should one be stubborn still,
climbing without a trail,
or join the gang on the hill
where success is certain and pale?

Reasons change like the breeze,
only vitality sweeps
some beyond hillocks and trees,
others into the deeps.

DIARY

The ice, for years like rock, was cracked in March,
and slowly snow, apparently secure,
re-formed and grew into an avalanche;
a trickle turned a sea that beat the shore

in changing rhythms, even at low tide,
a second heart-beat in the spring,
lightning and rain in place of ice and cloud—
the hours speak—a diary in song.

PACKAGED

Packaged feeling
with a label,
like "despair"
or "love" or "ache,"
looks appealing
on the table:
one can share
it like a cake.

Public prayer,
instant meal
sell if nicely
canned for retail;
but to care
what we feel
quite precisely
and in detail—

that is crude
and separates
like free use
of honest reason.
Eat your food
and clean your plates;
thoughts conduce
to hurt and treason.

ON TURNING FORTY

The years of hope and promise passed—
a spreading smile on water, then
a fleeting grin that turns
into reflection trembling with
the mockery of change.

No refuge in the future left,
no certainty of promise kept
though many broke and drowned,
and no clear image of a past
that grins and grows.

THEY

They lived before the fall,
their ignorance was rank,
their dirty towns were small,
their Gothic houses stank.

For every burning question
they had a wet reply;
if one attacked their bastion,
that heretic must die.

Doubt cracked their tidy walls,
and freedom is not neat;
those with the minds of thralls
prefer the old deceit.

Insight disturbs, the letter
is readily believed:
the less one sees, the better
is certainty achieved.

Freedom and doubt are twins,
and doubt exposes dirt.
They did not know their sins—
nor that the best things hurt.

THE SENTENCE

The sentence kills a frightened cry,
the truth dies in a stainless tract:
must tidy phrases falsify
the wild complexity of fact?

The witness speaks, and everyone
knows that the sentence has been just:
what *we* have felt and thought and done
is blacked out by devout disgust.

The guilty prisoner must die,
the witness all but saw the act.
Must tidy phrases falsify
the wild complexity of fact?

Or can bold language reach the beat
of dread against the sweaty skin,
the parched taste of unjust defeat,
the lightning bolt of the first sin?

Words did and can create the sky
we see, and life's mad cataract—
and language need not falsify
the wild complexity of fact.

RELIGION

I

They know how to deal with death
solemnly doling out dole
dolled up as for a play
pray-acting to draw tears
a few at a time
like grains of salt
spice
on the dry crumbs of life
something to talk of later
as one chats of a meal
the day we buried . . .
dolled up
solemn
know how.

II

They still know how to answer Job
and when sedative language fails
there are pills
and cells
to silence scream and vision
starched white to help flowing black
keep up the pretense of peace
lest anyone wake up
in the dark.

III

To know how to sleep in the dark
is religion.
What doth it profit man
to open his eyes in the night
and to see the dark
while most men dream?
Not all that scream
are prophets
but every prophet is mad.
The priests have always known that
and known how
to spice the dry crumbs
stuffing the mouth of Job.

IV

City of almost dry bones
where the not quite dead generation
waits for the trains and the trucks and the lime pits
starving and stinking in filth
patriarchs dying in gutters
and corpses piled high on wheel barrows.
Yisgadal v'yiskadash shmay rabo.
And the bones came together
bone to his bone
an exceeding great army.
Distant voices from buried worlds
grandfathers

and their fathers beyond them
straight backs
and stakes
and stiff necks
and soon
mountains of false teeth
an exceeding great army.
May The Great Name Magnify And Sanctify Itself.

V

Yisgadal v'yiskadash shmay rabo.
Triumph over the dust and filth of reality.
Sedative language
dreams in the dark.
But does anyone know
how to face the void?
What doth it profit to scream
when the heart is not eased
and eyes dry as bones
to wake those who sleep
and break up the play
for what?
Why rob the dust of its dignity
sleep of its dreams
and death of
Yisgadal v'yiskadash shmay rabo.

VI

Thou shalt not steal
faith from the filth that remains
and pills from the sick
but neither shalt thou bear false witness
or take in vain The Great Name.
And words that were triumph once
cried from the stake
are false in the face
of those piles of false teeth
and faith cannot whiten
the ovens and lime pits
and no incantation
can silence the scream
of Job.

VII

They know how to deal with deaths
a few at a time
something to talk of later
but not how to speak of this.
What shall we do when their play ends
even between acts
or when their lines are so palpably learned
and their holy tone hollow
and we see through the holes
into emptiness?

After the pray-act and
the spice and the vision
after the filth and the dust and
shantih shantih shantih and Zen
and profanity
no new incantation
or seduction
by ritual
language
or pills
only what some become
and the gift of new eyes
not for dreams and visions and refuge
eyes that see dust as dust
without blinking
and the will to endure and defy and prevail.

JULY

Slowly the moon
climbs through the leaves
and caresses my bed.
Gone is the day's oppressive heat.

Soon, very soon
all that now grieves
will be blissfully dead.
Never was sleeplessness so sweet.

SLOW SOLITUDE

Slow solitude of night
invades my days,
between my thought and sight
a growing space.

As in a dream, I lack
something to cross;
I like the wakeful dark
that hides my loss.

No wish, no hope, no urge,
I am resigned;
O slow, dark waves, submerge
a willing mind!

YET

Nights of pain to give birth
to a few lines.
Marvel that clods of earth
can produce signs.

If the song of a bird
never can teach,
whom could my wingless word
hope to reach?

Triumph that it is there,
far from the shore,
briefly in earless air!
Once I hoped more.

Early dreams have long drowned,
heard lines heard wrong,
cursed is all human sound,
yet I crave song.

BIRD

Bird with heavy marble wings,
cursed with feather dreams, am I:
though my spirit soars and sings,
I am mute and cannot fly.

Over never felt resistance
dreamless nightingales prevail,
unaware of azure distance,
while we marvel as we fail.

WORDS ARE LIKE INSECTS

Words are like insects: many crawl,
a few are butterflies, and more have wings;
but habits of their own have all—
some like to swarm, some dig, and some have stings.

To watch them fly and contemplate
the subtle iridescence of a noun,
one's color and another's weight,
is like a walk through an exotic town.

But to wed words to our will,
one has to wander far, turn stones, and find
both winged and creeping words until
each illustrates a passage of the mind.

FOR D

What you need is the gentle twilight
in which someone shares what you feel,
and not the glaring high light
on a computer's steel.

That I have felt what hurt you
and have survived, offends:
right now it would be virtue
to not quite comprehend,

to try to share the frightening
experience that is new,
expect a stroke of lightning,
and feel and think like you.

TO A READER

You think you hear *me* and look into my heart;
but I stand alone on a windswept beach
while somebody else is playing my part,
and I call and I strain and I cannot reach.

Yet sometimes you see me and ask to explain
the speeches I hate that you think are mine,
and you hate them, too, and I feel your disdain,
and silence sounds guilty and words are in vain.

Oh, where is the gesture, the Zen master's sign
to destroy the lit stage and reveal the dark beach,
to bring your eye to discover my line
and your ear to perceive—and dispense with—my speech?

LATE AUGUST

Is this the wind to break the summer's grip
and rout the damp dominion of his heat?
Is freedom summoned by this thunderclap,
and will cool rain restore strength to create?

The trees are lush, the vegetables flourish,
and insects breed and all the things that swarm:
I'd trade them all for one bright flash of courage;
O break the tyranny of summer, storm!

LEAP

From the searing sand of despair
dive into the cool sea of words
to wash off the world and dare
the freedom and music of birds!

Stranded life is impure;
abandon the broken shells:
the eagle that is mature
leaps into space and sails.

LOVE LETTER TO A DAUGHTER

We were climbing a wave-licked cliff
and you would not beware of the whirl.
Forget me: what would you do if
I were dead and you had a girl—

and your warning is scorned and she mocks
your loving dread and won't learn
how to scale the slippery rocks,
and she stumbles at every turn

and gets angry when you hold the rope
though it gives her another chance,
and she screams that she wants more scope,
and where she can't stand wants to dance.

Don't think I don't know how you feel
as if I had never been young:
I know that the rope feels like steel,
and learning takes always too long.

But think for just one night: what should
a father or mother do?
A thousand thoughts are no good;
I am ready to listen to you.

One sleepless night might be worth
a year of discussions and rules;
O my darling, my darling, the earth
is dark enough without fools!

RIDE

On the train just to ride and look—
oh, to leave behind and to move,
skimming villages like a book,
and eyes as one might read of love—

riding, skimming, leaving behind,
faces get on, distraught;
turning the page of a mind,
glimpsing a passing thought—

reading without being there,
oh, without, without any aim;
faces get off in despair,
blur, and look almost the same.

And if I went back, just to ride,
and left and got off some place,
wherever, to get outside:
should I, should I have a face?

GOETHE'S CRITICS

Why does Herr Geheimrat scatter
his talents (as rain is by God),
when I do so much better
           and plod?

It certainly is a flaw
when a man wastes nights and days,
after first having studied law,
           on plays.

He's a statesman, yet tries his hand
at novels, and he neglects
our glorious duchy and
           directs.

A poet may be a lover,
but science he should leave alone,
and least of all should discover
           a bone.

If he had only stuck
to lyrical poetry,
he might have gone far with luck,
           like me!

A MIND AGAINST MADNESS

When lightninglike blindness
builds black walls
between two that walk,
and though they see woods, path, and bridge,
and even the trees of each other's speech,
they suddenly cannot find
the wood of the mind,
and darkness dims day
as a world is drowned,
and no goodness can breach sudden solitude:

let language sing
to no ear, no aim,
a bridge for the heart to leap,
a naked, new-born cry in the night,
as a child might weep at mind's end,
where prayer helps some
and a canvas or marble others,
to ease what no scream, tears, head against rock
could quiet:

sing not a thought that was there before,
but a mind against madness,
a heart breaking inrushing darkness
lightninglike
language that burns in the mind.

UNSHELTERED

Unsheltered, shivering nights,
ice in the soul, aglitter,
alive with endless lights;
venom that is not bitter,

glistening effervescence,
crystals that cut what they blind
with the witty iridescence
of an unsheltered mind;

and the space of an ocean of snow
pierced by peaks that the marbled sea
whipped by hurricanes does not know,

beyond hazes, almost above breath,
the sun-drenched chastity
of brotherhood with death.

AN INVOCATION

Not only velvet stars of edelweiss
have marked my way when every trail was lost,
but also jagged rocks, spires of ice,
and bodies felled by frost.

You can grow gentians bluer than the sky
in pots, but can you feel the seventh day
of wind, no water? Let me try
not to strew flowers but recall a way.

Not hothouse blossoms cut from thorny stems,
curiosities raised under glass and fit
to decorate a table, nor strange gems,
triumphs of craftsmanship so exquisite

that no one could infer the mine's deep night
in which despair, seeking survival, tore
the stones from rock: no, less to give delight
than to crack walls and open up a door.

MY GOD

A girl with blind and oozing eyes
tied to some Indian tree to beg,
her lovely features black with flies,
mosquitoes on her leg—

her night untouched by dusk, some brute
raped her forgotten body: did
that darkness scream? or was it mute
like God, who hid?

Having kept silent is the sin
against the spirit: Judas' kiss
dared more—and could my God have been
guilty of cowardice?

Oh, if my God had lived! Yours did,
but they are phantoms, not divine,
or silent monsters: your gods hid,
not mine!

FOG

Fog sees the trees through half-closed eyes
and weaves the street into a dream.
Fog is remembrance become peace.
Why does the sun shine in my mind?

HOW FAR IS FAR?

I'm going *pur*ty far, she said—
white sweater and blue overalls,
her face turned up, her little head
topped off with sunny curls.

In Potiphar's accursed bed
Joseph refused and went to jail:
he would not go so far, instead
went far beyond his goal.

How far is far? The coveted
field's edge? or doing as we feel?
Far is beyond the edge of dread,
past hope, sustained by will.

Oh, pretty far is quite well bred
and pretty as a puzzling smile,
but far lies where no tears are shed,
the other side of hell.

SIR

(For Martha Linde)

They called me Sir, asking the way,
which was both pertinent and prudent,
provided only that they knew
that I was not, like them, a student.

But how did they, lost as they were,
perceive my temporality,
my Who and What, and call me Sir,
when I was not aware of me?

Am I my job? am I my age?
am I my skin? I have no core:
Man is the verse and not the stage,
the restless water, not the shore.

DÉJÀ VU

When life turns into films that we have seen,
and others, when they laugh or talk or grieve,
seem like dull actors on a distant screen,
we wonder if the time has come to leave;

while in another age we should have been
revered as wise and deemed fit to receive
such honors as one shows a king or queen,
and all but we should have been thought naive.

AUTUMN

Hard is the maple's wood,
unbending the trunk, almost grey,
buried in darkness the roots,
a tree among trees in May.

Touched by the autumn frost
when the birds no longer sing,
the leaves about to be lost
outdazzle the plumage of spring.

Even the sunlight was dull
till it struck their weightless form:
what matter that soon they fall,
carried away in a storm?

LOVE

Love is the lingering of the heart
in little traits and incidents,
the mind's caress of every part
that touched a reminiscent sense.

It dwells on trifles as on passion,
on details un-love thinks absurd,
transforms all things and likes to fashion
worlds out of nothing but a word.

Playful, imprudent, it decides
to live completely insecure,
and like the never sleeping tides,
love grows the power to endure.

AMOS' IMMORTAL COW

Attractive by the grace of hooks,
her mammal breasts are strapped to bask
in unbelieving, lustful looks;
her mammal mind behind a mask

of cheap, but not yet instant, charm,
her bovine brows are never creased:
O cow of Bashan, go to farm,
you are not woman but a beast.

CHURCH SUPPER

Since *Angst* has become popular
we do admire Kierkegaard,
but don't care for his either/or:

instead of choosing, we prefer
to cite Freud, Marx, and Heidegger,
mix history with sex and care,

and advertise a smorgasbord
to fill the house of our Lord.

RIDDLE

Who can by stunning exegesis
prove absolutely any thesis?
A sweeping lack of common sense
he compensates with confidence.

He answers questions with old quotes
and, when in doubt, tells anecdotes.
His voice is soothing, smooth, and round,
designed expressly to expound
what, without unction, would astound
because it plainly is not sound.

His most exciting exegeses
depend on flagrant catachreses,
and none can match his eminence
in misusing both *thus* and *hence*.

HOW MANY HOURS?

How many hours have slowly dripped into
a placid past and lost their fleeting shape?
Peaceful and smooth now, they cast back a view
that freezes me beyond hope of escape.

Not always prodigal and aimless, I
reached for some drops falling into the lake,
as if my longing could solidify;
but work is merely restless sleep; we wake,

and all we did turns into dreams that drown,
when our eyes are opened, in the past.
Unable to arrest what hurtles down,
we are yet free to love what does not last.

THE BURNING BUSH

I

Iron clouds,
heavy and dark,
are cracked by sun rays
that kindle trees.

Fall's forests burn
like Moses' bush.

Mountains in silent flames,
but no voice.

Fall's fever blazes
for days,
and at night the moon skiff
glides over golden foliage.

II

Treacherous to the end,
life hides her decay,
dyes death itself
like swarms of butterflies.

Minds take wing,
touched by cold fire,

the spreading desert
forgotten,

and flutter caresses,
senseless, luminous love,
but there is
no voice.

III

When the desert drowns
in blindness,
and sand unseen
yields to yellow and scarlet,

tenderness covers
the rot of treachery,

language lulls
pain to sleep,

poetry touches
the skin of
dying life
and shudders.

IV

Oak leaves turn copper
with touches
of patina
and red sparks.

Maple leaves
shine like brass

but translucent and voiceless
like insect wings.

Dogwood leaves,
no kin of spring's blossoms,
are dark and intense
as childhood.

V

Summers one sees and can count,
and the frost
one expects
like night.

Winter one awaits
like white thunder,

but the splendor
of fall

is lightning
piercing the peace
of hearts
ready for darkness.

VI

Expectations return
for the capping clap,
like a stupid child
with closed eyes.

Brutal memory knows
there is no voice.

Like the bush I burn
without relief,

waiting like inert wood,
but there was no clap even then,
nor peace, nor darkness
till the voice had come from the bush.

INTERLUDE:
TEN GERMAN POEMS

(1939–42)

YELLOWSTONE

Da wo das Wasser in Kaskaden
versprühend in die Tiefe rauscht
hab ich dem Strom so manche Stunde
versonnen und verträumt gelauscht.

Das Wasser grub sich ins Gestein
wo es in grauser Schlucht sich windet
aus der der Fels in tausend Türmen
den Weg zur Sonne aufwärts findet.

Im Traume folgte ich dem Strome
durch Wald und Wüste immer hin
und sah die Welt im Strom gelöst
jenseits von allem Ziel und Sinn.

KRIEGSAUSBRUCH, 1939

Wohl strahlt die Sonne über reifen Feldern
und Früchte hängen schwer von jedem Ast,
die letzten Rosen blühn, die Wälder duften,
   und niemals war die Welt so schön.

Doch keine Hände greifen nach den Früchten,
das Korn steht ungeschnitten und verdirbt,
und all die Blumen welken ungesehen,
   freudlos und ohne Liebe hin.

Und nur im Traume küss ich ihre Blüten
und nehm die Früchte in die durstgen Hände
und frage auch wohl einmal ob ein Sommer
   wie dieser jemals wiederkommt.

KEIN GOTT

Mir gab kein Gott von meinem Leid zu singen
und keine Sprache formte meinen Schmerz:
wie sollte je ein Menschenohr begreifen
was doch mein eignes Herz nicht fasst?

Wie lange habe ich mich selbst belogen
und meinen eignen Sinn betört
und sprach von längst vergällten Freuden
und lächelte und lachte meiner Qual!

Ich fing mein Herz in tausend bunten Träumen
und zog es lockend von der Wirklichkeit
und lebt im Spiel und alten Sagen
wo Hunger war und Frost und viele starben.

Doch alles jenes ward mir zu "erlebtem"
zu einem selbst geformten grossen Bilde
und alle Schmerzen halfen mitgestalten
was einst lebendig auferstehen sollte.

Ich selber war das Kolossalgebilde
um das die wirren Träume kreisten;
und waren sie auch immer neu verschieden
ich selber fehlte doch in keinem.

Ich aber glaubte glühend an die Wahrheit
der tausendfarbgen Fieberphantasien
und was ich schuf um meine Qual zu lindern
ward mir Vision und heiliges Gebet.

Und dennoch fühlt ich alle jene Schmerzen
kein Traum war tief genug sie zu betäuben:
ich schaute doch mit fieberirren Augen
und hörte gellend jeden Schmerzensschrei.

Oh zähle nicht die Leiden die ich schaute
und nicht die Qualen die mein Ohr vernahm;
verkünde nichts von dem was ich getragen
da ich geträumt, gelacht, geliebt.

Denn Rede kann die Schmerzen nicht mehr lindern
und Sprache macht das schwere Herz nicht leicht;
die Jahre gingen da noch Tränen halfen
das Herz von Qualen rein zu waschen.

Längst hab ich fest in meiner Brust verschlossen
was immer mir an Schmerzen wiederfuhr
bis ich die letzte Qual nicht länger fasste:
da hat mein Herz sich berstend aufgetan

die Wände schmolzen und die Mauern fielen
und dieser Schrei fuhr in die taube Welt.
Verstumme nun und schliesse deine Lippen
und lache bis dein Herz zerspringt!

STIMMEN

Siehst du am Hang vom Sturm gebeugt die Föhren
wie Menschen ob der Last von vielen Jahren?
Hast du des Nachts die Berge rufen hören
da Sturm und Donner lang verklungen waren?

Ich habe ihren Ruf in mancher Nacht
da er in Qualen barst zutiefst erfahren
und habe in der Dunkelheit gewacht
und meinte dass die Berge Gott gebaren.

Du kennst die Stimme jener Nächte nicht
und meinst dass Berge nicht zu rufen wissen;
du meinst ich hätte nur ein Traumgesicht:
dein Herz hat nie ihr geller Schrei zerrissen.

Nur jene können ihre Sprache fassen
in deren Herzen solche Qualen leben
die sich von Menschenlaut nicht formen lassen
und denen dann die Berge Stimme geben.

ALLMÄCHTGER GOTT

Allmächtger Gott der Du das All erfasst
und Dich in Erde, Himmel, Wald und Auen
in letzter Herrlichkeit verwirklicht hast
dass wir Dich stets in allen Dingen schauen

Unendlicher der diese ganze Welt
mit Glanz erfüllt und ohne Grenzen ist
und alles Lebens Glut in sich enthält:
wer zweifelte dass Du vollendet bist?

Ich glaub an Dich selbst wenn ich voller Qual
verzweifelt rasend Deinem Namen fluche.
Wärst Du nicht wären Schmerz und Freude schal;
doch weiss ich nicht: Bist Du es den ich suche?

Unendlichkeit ist lieblos und Vollendung
gebiert nicht Kraft und schöpferischen Willen;
Vollkommnen fehlen Prophetie und Sendung
und wer nie sehnte kann kein Sehnen stillen.

Und dennoch find ich Dich auf allen Wegen:
die Berge leben und es spricht das Meer
und alle Wesen atmen Deinen Segen
und wären ohne Dich flach, seicht und leer.

Doch erst im Menschen schuf sich Gott den Geist
der schaffend die Unendlichkeit erfasst;
da ihn sein Sehnen in die Ferne weist
sucht, liebt und wirkt er ohne Rast.

So ward die Gottheit die sich in der Welt
noch tatlos schlummernd ohne Schaffenslust
in herrlichster Vollendung dargestellt
im Menschen erst der eignen Kraft bewusst.

STERNENSCHICKSAL

Ich bin der Sterne einer die im Weltenraum
ewig allein die vorgeschriebne Bahn verfolgen:
um mich ist Nacht und unermesslich grosse Kälte
in mir ist Licht und Glut. Ich strahle da ich brenne.

Doch lebt in mir ein Traum der grösser ist als ich
ein Märchen das mir meine Mutter einst ersann:
dass über uns am Himmel eine Sonne ist
von deren Licht und Glut wir nur ein Spiegel sind.

Es ist ein irrer Traum denn für die Nacht allein
hat mich mein Gott erschaffen und bestimmt
dass ich den anderen im finstern Dunkel leuchte
dass sie dem eignen Weg die Treue halten.

Doch wenn der Horizont dereinst im Licht erglüht
dann werd ich wissen dass die Sonne sich verkündet:
mein Traum war wahr und wird sich bald erfüllen
doch ich verbrenn im Lichte eh der Morgen graut.

EPITAPH

Alles starb in meinem Herzen
was nicht reines Feuer war:
in den Gluten meiner Qualen
bracht ich's Gott im Himmel dar.

Nur das flammenhafte Sehnen
das sich grad am Brande nährt
hat die Gluten überstanden
noch nachdem sie Gott verzehrt.

MARIA

Selbst in der Mutter abgehärmten Zügen
erscheint sein Abbild tierhaft nur und trübe:
sind beide auch voll Sehnen und voll Liebe
weiss er wie Gleichnisse und Ähnlichkeiten trügen.

Malt sich der Sonne Bild in einem Teich
so ähnelt all ihr Licht und ihre Glut
mehr ihrem lauen Bilde in der Flut
und ist sein göttlich Wesen ihr viel wen'ger gleich.

Wohl hat sie ihn in ihrem Leib getragen
und nährte seinen Leib von ihrem Herzen;
den Geist gebar er sich aus eignen Schmerzen
und schuf die Lippen die nun Gottes Worte sagen.

Was weiss sie davon? Ihr Los scheint ihr schwer!
Gezisch: er predigt ohne Unterlass—
ist ledig—Huren—Zöllner—dies und das.
Er muss zurück! Ihr Antlitz aufgeregt und leer.

Er kennt sie und er sieht die Menge gaffen
doch glaubt er ob sie ihn auch arg verschreien
an einen Geist-geeinten Bund der Freien
und donnert: Weib, was habe ich mit dir zu schaffen?

SONNENUNTERGANG

Lang schon liegen der düsteren Städte
himmelstürmende Kathedralen,
Stein gewordene Inbrunst der Väter,
von den Schatten der Nacht umfangen.
Nur noch die Kuppen der höchsten Berge
die einst im Lichte des jungen Tages
Gottes Erscheinung bebend erschauten
zucken im letzten Lichte des Abends.

Farbig glühende Wolken entgleiten
müde ins purpurne Dunkel der Nacht
und des Himmels prächtigstes Schauspiel
löst sich schon zitternd im Meere auf:
Feuer sprühende Wogen jauchzen
donnernd der sinkenden Sonne entgegen
aber noch eh sie im Tiefen verrollen
werfen sie schaudernd ein letztes Echo
mächt'ger Akkorde vom Abgrund zurück;
mahnen an trunkene Symphonien
tiefstes Abbild der eigenen Seele.
Neu erstehen vergangene Zeiten
Verse umschweben das bangende Herz
deuten auf Träume verflogener Stunden—
und schon neigt sich der Sonnenwagen
in den lachenden Abgrund der Nacht.
Zügle die Rosse oh ewiger Vater!
Siehe ich will nicht im Dunkel ertrinken
während noch Jugend mich strahlend umloht.
Und schon eil ich auf feurigen Fluten
Deinem Gespanne mächtig entgegen.

Aus dem Reigen der sprühenden Wogen
reck ich die Arme und greif in die Speichen:
kann ich der Sonne Wagen nicht wenden
nicht ihn verzögern ein Menschenalter
selbst noch im Glanze des Lichtes zu leben—
bin ich der letzte des alten Geschlechtes
will ich gerädert vom Schicksal verderben.

REGEN

Der Regen ist ein müdes Kind
das heim zur Mutter Erde will:
er gleitet schlafend durch den Wind
und sinkt zur Erde und liegt still.

REMBRANDT
AND OTHER POEMS

(1940–60)

EXILE (1940)

This was my land before you came.
For both of us it was too small.
I left, but I expect to tell
one day the story of your fall.

A WOMAN'S LOVE SONG

(After a German Version of an Egyptian Poem, about 1500 B.C.)

I do what my heart wishes
when I lie in your arms.
To see you is light for my eyes.
I cling to you because I see your love,
you that are great in my heart.
The hours of my life are filled with eternity
since I sleep with you.
You raised up my heart
when it was in night.

I am your first sister.
I am the piece of land
that you planted with flowers.—
Pleasant is the pond your hand shaped in it
and in the chill of the north wind
the beautiful place where we walk
when your hand lies in mine.
My heart is saturated with joy
since we walk together.
It is wine for me to hear your voice.
I live because I hear it.

KABIR

*(From Otto von Glasenapp's German Version
of a Poem written around 1500 A.D.)*

To what avail do you ascend the tower?
God is not deaf, he will perceive you here.
You call the faithful to implore his power?
Search for him in your heart, replies Kabir.

HEART BEAT

I feel my heart beat.
Time flies
like splinters of marble
into the air.
Soon the figure is cut,
the chisel rests.
What will remain?

THE CONDUCTOR

Though he is old his eyes betray
that he relives the scorching hell
and ecstasy that found their way
into the score his hands compel.
His fingers mold the sound like clay
and with one gesture they can tell
a movement's temper or allay
an outburst that no god could quell.

What the whole orchestra conveys
a-thousand-voiced while every soul
projects itself in what it plays
he comprehends in his control
and *is* what all the others say:
the incarnation of the whole.

REMBRANDT

Deep crimson velvet lined with ermine fur,
pictures of women's breasts and eager thighs
seem dull and dead before the sunken eyes
of my creations: beggars whom you slur,

the poor, the old, the Jews—the scum that crowds
into the fringes of your wealthy towns:
Without the benefit of purple gowns,
or naked bodies under silken shrouds,

without a multicolored interplay,
I model them out of the dark of night,
bring them to life with but a beam of light,
as God created us from dirt and clay.

The mud-brown portrait of some beggar sage,
a little etching, all restraint and quiet,
contains more life than all the Baroque riot
and infinite contortions of this age.

OCCUPATION

Parading among a conquered and starving people
among the ruins
with patches and stripes and ribbons and hash marks
one for a year in the army
for having grown callous and dumb
one for a year in the States
for learning to goldbrick and pass the buck
one for the fight and one for the occupation
for drinking and whoring and black marketeering
one for the victory that is melting away
while they parade among the ruins with ribbons and stripes.

THE LEPER

His nose rotted away, his lion face
disfigured to inhuman majesty,
the leper lifts his staff and cries: *Tamay!*
Sacred and cursed am I, beware of me,
living destruction of the human form,
more fearful than a corpse, for I live on,
a curse on the Creator's vaunted grace.

The Law is for the living, not for us.
We are the brinks of life, we and the dead
and women who give birth, we are *tamay*,
unclean, and banished from the sanctuary.
Growth and decay are yet beyond the Law.
My face, like His, must not be seen by man:
hide in a cleft, my glory passes by.

THE CURTAIN

The curtain arches in the breeze
a waterfall's suspended motion
no past or future but the ease
and self-containment of the ocean.

And who could say it is at rest
or moving? It is frozen fire
the gesture of a woman's breast
that curves and stills without desire.

OLD LETTERS

A flimsy footbridge over the abyss
of an unfathomable gorge of rock,
the fright and feel of death, the precipice
of my own mind, a sense of guilt and shock.

Voices I thought—or did I hope?—had died
plead from the depths within where I had sought
to bury them. For years they tried
to pierce my memory and reach a thought.

Some sound more urgent now than when I read
them first. Some, so condensed, despair. But all
live and accuse. Not they, my mind was dead.
Down there is life, my footing gives, I fall.

HOW DOES ONE GROW?

How does one grow to greatness like a sun
or arch one's soul beyond all petty things
to form a sky untouched by evenings
indifferent but benign and wholly one?

Does beauty burst from listening within
or do buds strain to feel the coming flower?
How does a living thing gain timeless power?
By meditation or through work and sin?

All those who follow formulas may glow
with faith's quick paper-nourished fire;
that which endures is not earned by desire
but falls to one who does not cease to grow.

THE OPENED HEART

To live with an opened-up heart
that the wind may rush in and the air
and the light and space become part
of my soul and my life and I share

in all that is vast and free
in the breath of the night and the sky
and the darkness is mine and the tree
is not a reproach but I.

In the branches I rise, in the leaves
I sleep in the wind, and the trunk
is my strength, and the cloud that grieves
gives me rain and makes me drunk.

NIETZSCHE

I

To write, my eyes on what is wide and silent,
and bring to bear the brilliance of the sky
upon man's narrow hell—the twisting lanes
of human thought where garbage of the mind
is left to rot, attracting human flies
that feast on waste and seek the warmth of age.

They breed in filth and deify the sweet
cadaver of a mutilated Jew.

The wasted body on the Roman gallows,
the furtive logic of the catacombs
that once stunned unwashed slaves, drugged by the fumes
of decomposing corpses, thrilling too
some of the rich, a new debauchery,
no longer is the brothel of the heart,
a new lust sought in twilight, but divine.

Segesta's temple on the hill abandoned,
a radiant ruin—sky and wind and light—
and Siracusa's columns, wide and silent,
linked with thick walls shut out the sky: a church.

They breed in filth and deify the sweet
cadaver of a mutilated Jew.

II

The lake leaps at the rock, and green and grey
are pure and hard as ice swept by the sun.
I see, I swim, I climb, I soar
like wind over the Alpine snows.

To catch the wind and air and ice in prose,
to let my language, like that lake, reflect
the freedom of the mountains—to create
a choice between the sunless romance of
men's writhing alleys and the dawn of day.

DO NOT PRAY

The branches do not pray, but I
am almost moved to imitate their thrust
by raising my arms blindly to the sky,
neither in thanks nor, least of all, in trust—
no, not to beg and bend or pray and preach
but, like this tree, to leave behind the earth
in which I too am rooted and to reach
into sheer air: radiance and heedless mirth,
abandonment without all faith or hope,
the freedom of a gesture without aim,
a slanting dance of blossoms, or a trope
that breaks a context and resolves a tension—
a protest, a delight, a dying flame
that seeks an uninhabited dimension.

GOD

The partner of a passion that transcends
the crude embrace of words, the groping stammer
of flesh, and the response that comprehends—
a thrust beyond the tidy world of grammar,

beyond relationships, however tender,
an act of passion that a life sustains;
there is no partner—a complete surrender,
wholehearted madness that no creed explains.

Whipped by despair, torn by the tasks that hound us,
half drugged by repetition, loath to plod
and play by tedious turns, we scream to reach, to be
beyond the sane inane things that surround us
and somersault beyond conformity,
but fall back and lose all when we say God.

IN HEINE'S TRACES

I

Humor and passion
are not opposite:
to deflate fashion,
reason needs wit.

II

Graven images are grave
in the region of the Nile,
Christ says he alone can save,
but the Buddha has a smile.

III

If the world was made on purpose
and there was no faulty staffing,
disagreement, or subversion,
surely, God must still be laughing.

NOVEMBER

What once kept me sleepless
no longer matters.
The burning foliage
the fall wind scatters.

The blazes are choked
by November's chill.
I welcome the frost
but am burning still.

Yesterday's flames
are like yesterday's breath.
But I shall burn
and love it till death.

And if God choose
burn better after.

MORE SATIRICAL VERSE

(1947–69)

SOMEBODY ELSE'S GRASS

The child believes the grown-up can
do what he likes, and envies him;
but if you ask the grown-up man,
the child can follow every whim.

The pupil wishes he could teach;
the teacher, he might sit and doze:
each is exasperating each,
and no one likes the status quos.

THE MODERN HOUSE

No room to read or weep or pray:
an area to live, an ell to eat,
a space to watch TV, a place to play,
a kitchen that is practically complete
with chemically treated floor,
a so-called room for the whole family,
but only two rooms with a closing door—
the other for utility.

READING
THE UNSILENT GENERATION

An Anonymous Symposium in which Eleven College Seniors
[Princeton '57] *Look at Themselves and Their World* [1958]

> What bothers me is not that you're strange
> but that you have no desire to change.
> That you're odd I should not give a damn
> if you did not say: "That's how I am:
>
> My home was like this, my parents like that,
> so how can I help it if I am a brat?
> I guess I was brainwashed to think as I do,
> and I hope to brainwash my children too.
>
> I am not very prejudiced, only
> without certain faults one tends to be lonely.
> I am irrational but well-dressed,
> and my education was the best.
>
> I see myself as a club candidate:
> I may be noisy, but I am first-rate;
> I have done nothing special, but I made the race.
> I look at myself as a kind of a case."
>
> Is there nothing to which you would give yourself?
> You are finished, a stuffed bird that waits on a shelf,
> an exhibit without any dream or dread:
> before you have lived you are proud to be dead.

TEENAGER

Kids are so cool
and grownups so dumb;
Mom is a fool
and Dad is a bum.

I am so hip
and you are so square;
I take a trip
and you pay the fare.

You are way out
and getting grey;
I am a lout
and like it that way.

LO-KU*

SOCIOLOGIST'S LOVE SONG

Oh, infinite sublimity
of maximal proximity!

DIALOGUE

No time for dialogue,
the age of the diagram:
they worship blueprint and hog
while they talk of the cross and the lamb.

WHEN

When a guru can can kangaroos
and a kangaroo can can a guru
and a kangaroo can cancan
then a guru will need mantan.

---

*Jeanette Mirsky's coinage.

ANOTHER RIDDLE

Who denounced hypocrites at home
and priests whose conduct was unsavory,
not the atrocities of Rome,
torture and slavery?

> Injustice to the poor and strangers
> enraged him less than money changers
> too near the temple: where we fail
> in his eyes is the rummage sale.

A lustful look concerned him more
than mass murder and exploitation;
he did not preach an end to war,
he preached salvation.

THEODICY

Why did God make hemorrhoids?
    To love the light we need the dark
and girls with adenoids
    enhance the song of the lark.

DOUBTS ABOUT FREUD

Why don't we dare wish what is pleasant?
If dreams project our secret wishes
why do I never get a present?
Could my desires be that pernicious?

Why don't we wake elated by
successes day will never see?
In dreams I fare far worse than I
have yet done in reality.

A CROWD OF THOUSANDS

(After *The New York Times*)

Here's five bucks he will.
                              Aw, he wants to live.
You're chicken, that's what.
                              Gee, what a fuss!
I hope he'll jump soon...
                              What odds do you give?
...because if he don't we'll miss the last bus.

THE ACADEMIC ZOO

Each of them knows its lightless hole
better than any other mole.

Most birds soar through the ether, but
since peacocks cannot fly they strut.

How snug the little spiders look:
each sits forever in its nook.

Whatever spins web or cocoon
is welcome, however jejune.

> Butterfly
> need not apply.

A LIGHT-HEARTED GUIDE
TO SOME CLASSICS

(1961)

ANTIGONE

*As Read by a Social Worker**

Did Antigone have a tragic flaw?
She got into trouble with the law.

Her father was also her big half-brother,
and she was born to her own grandmother.

Her father had clubbed his father's head,
until her grandfather was quite dead.

Her mother committed suicide,
and her father, upset, became one-eyed.

A moment later he became totally blind,
all of which might have disturbed a lesser girl's mind.

But she took care of the invalid,
loved one of her brothers and was a sweet kid.

But a vow-breaking cheat was her eldest brother,
and the two boys fought and killed each other.

Then her uncle, alias great-uncle, said
that the liar was good and her favorite bad,

---

*For a different reading, see my *Tragedy and Philosophy*.

and proclaimed a big funeral for the cheat,
leaving the other corpse for the dogs to eat.

Antigone did not find life so much fun
and risked it to bury her father's son.

She was not mixed up, as she well might have been;
and when proposed to, she was not keen.

Her suitor was her cousin in more ways than one,
and she was not eager to bear his son.

Antigone had no tragic flaw:
she had reasons for defying the law
and for hanging herself—jes like her Ma.

TANTALUS' TRIBE

Even the Greeks thought eating one's children was odd,
but little Pelops was a dish fit for a god—

or so his father thought and cut him up
and served him to the gods when they gathered to sup.

The gods did not like the dinner and hurled
Tantalus into the underworld,

surrounding him with tasty dishes
that even he found more delicious,

but when he reached, whatever he was after
withdrew amid gales of Olympic laughter.

Not satisfied, the cruel gods collected
the limbs of Pelops, he was resurrected,

and in due time had sons. The rest is
still worse. The younger son, Thyestes,

had children with the wife of brother Atreus,
who then fell back on Tantalus' great ruse

and served his brother his adulterous brood.
Thyestes, unaware, enjoyed the food,

then fled in horror and begot
with his own daughter—if or not

he knew she was, the Greeks could not agree—
Aegisthus, worthy of his ancestry.

Exposed at birth by his affronted mother,
he was adopted by Thyestes' brother,

Atreus, who was revengeful still
and duly sent the boy to kill

Thyestes; but *he* recognized his boy
and told him it was better to destroy

the house of Atreus. Atreus' younger son
had married Helen, who found Paris fun

and went with him to live in Troy.
The Greeks chose Atreus' elder boy,

King Agamemnon, to lead them in war
against the Trojans. Gathered at the shore,

they had no wind to sail. There was a price,
a priest explained: the king must sacrifice

his daughter, young Iphigenia.
He did, and she went up in fire.

The Greeks left. Agamemnon's wife was furious.
Enter Aegisthus, hateful and injurious.

He comforted poor Clytemnestra and,
in Agamemnon's absence, ruled his land.

For ten years, Ae and Cly went steady.
When Ag returned, his bath was ready,

the lovers gave the king a bloody scrub,
and Atreus' son expired in the tub.

Orestes, son of Agamem and Cly,
decided that his mother had to die,

killed her, but then the son of Aga
felt guilty and, alas, went gaga.

Even the gods, though obviously tough,
now felt the joke had gone quite far enough,

forgave the boy and gave their protégé worth
by wedding Aga's son to Rita Hayworth.*

---

*According to some ancient authors, Orestes, after further bloodshed, married Hermione, his cousin, Helen's daughter, whose existence, however, is much less well attested than Hayworth's; and one school, not including the present author, believes that Hayworth was Helen's daughter, or even Helen herself; but the literature on all these questions is much too vast, so to say, to be summarized here, and it can only be hoped that the clarifications attempted in the present text, above, may lead the reader to an increased appreciation of the import, by no means only symbolical, of at least some of the relationships which, no doubt, on account of, or, as one might also, perhaps better, put it, because of their after all considerable complexity, have, unfortunately, all too often, if one may be bold enough to put it that way, not been fully, or at any rate not altogether (and this is important!) understood.

TABOO

(1962–69)

THE TABOOBOO SONG

For Allen Ginsberg

Tabu
was a blue
word on yellow cloth
under Freud

Tabúbu
boo bóo to
to tó tem
boo the taboo
bóo boo taboo

Taboo
was dont do
and dont think
dó do dont dáre
to speak or to think
before Freud

Taboo was a word
were some words
were some thoughts
were some acts
boo boo séx
homosexual sex
boo boo sexual
tátata tátata
bóo boo boo
sex

Tatathágata
Buddha
bóo boo taboo
Tathágata Buddha
bóo boo taboo
before Buddha
Boo boo béards
boo boo bárds
bearded bards
with their feet
on a cloth
boo the taboo
and sing of the Buddha

Nó one boos sex
homosexual sex
booboosexual beards
do not boo
and the bards
oh the bards
breák the taboos

Taboo is a word
on a boo boo book
Taboo is a word
and no longer a fact

Taboo is for boors
no longer for bards
and there are no boos
there are no taboos
only words
and facts
and sexual acts
kindness
and words
and music

tátata tátata
Buddha
Tathágata
Buddha
dádada dádada
Buddha

JUDGMENT

Lord of the storm that destroyed,
huddled and helpless, my people,
mocking their graceless death
with bird song and splendor of blossoms:

Lord of lightning that struck not
impious butcher kings,
saving his wrath for the masses
and his love for sunsets and trees:

Lord, if you came to judgment
and I had to sentence your soul,
weighing your rainbows and glaciers
against the mountains of bones,

Lord, you might yet win acquittal
if only the dead had beheld
glories on which you squandered
love that they never felt.

THE PRINCE

The prince that you saw crowned when early fall
has softened summer, rocking memory
to peaceful dreams, lies in the soil of spring.
O blabbering, scattering crowds: Nature awakes—
while you, the dust of the procession on
still sleeping faces, smile and babble of
what even you forget when morning comes
to crush you in an agony of light.

WORMS

Worms granted sight complain they were thrown into
　darkness,
children of angels, not dazzling thrusts from the slime;
conquerors of peaks see the sky and fable a fall,
stoutly denying their unseen climb.

DESERT-BORN GOD

Desert-born god,
sandstorm-cradled:
thine is burning,
blistering justice,
fiery darkness
that blinds and destroys.

Language, lead me not
windlike to praise him:
rhythms, swallow not
sight and memory,
lest I yield to him,
singing in darkness!

Memory, strike
through worshipful night:
rise like the sea wind,
purging the air!

Trees that are kissing
sand-whirling ground,
loving the storm that
snaps their trunks:
I shall not bow to
merciless glory.

Silvery circle,
sun rests in the storm,
the sound of the wind
is like heavy wine:
music, seduce me not
lest I forget!

Let not beauty
bury the past:
memory, marry
the flesh of god's glory!

Thine is the desert
in which you are buried,
thine is the darkness
that was your mother,
thine is the power
whose death I sing.

SUCCESS STORY

Slowly he learned how to cover his pages more quickly,
pausing no longer in desperate muteness not knowing
where next to hammer the rock in search of an opening:

Dimness his day and no longer a curse to vanquish;
details he once was the first to interpret in twilight—
wrongly perhaps, but the first—are his world and seem
  brilliant
clues to all shapes that people the dusk of his den.

Doubt is as distant to him as the nightmares of childhood.

Once every step was uncertain and seeing a triumph;
now he works fast while reclining and is not distracted
by what his eyes might report, for all is familiar:

And as his message is simple, bewildered millions
flock to its confident promise and relish its dimness,
eager for comfort. Reclining, he rocks them to sleep.

DREAMS

    A hall
        of warped
and cracked
    mirrors

    sneering
from walls
      whose intermittent
      darkness

  gives no
      reprieve
          to lidless
              eyes.

FOX

Lone streak of pride
    setting a course of grace
    weightlessly leading
    unloved
        always ahead of the pack:

Dream not red fox that you change
    dogs to become like you
    mind them not
        freedom is yours
        fox till you die
            till you die!

THE FALL

November 22, 1963

We fall like leaves
that drowse and drop,
and any grief
that outlives winter
drowns in the heedless
floods of spring.

Few fall like oaks,
breaking the branches
of some that stood near,
leaving a space
that many a summer
fails to fill.

Your fall,
like Agamemnon's,
shook the earth;
beyond the seas
strange women wailed
in empty terror.

Like Agamemnon,
you were a man
until you fell—
power and faults
more than replaceable.
Then, all at once,

your fall was hardly
some man's whom fate
had briefly raised,
one who survived
an endless war
and now leaves orphans:

Agamemnon dead
was not that king,
no, not the man
Achilles loathed,
sacker of cities
treading purple robes,

one who conceivably
deserved to die—
as who does not?—
and fated anyway:
as if a few
years mattered.

Pity is dwarfed by terror:
leaves we behold
as through a glass,
wistful and distant,
and even the oak
is a stranger.

Your fall crashed the glass:
though the seasons
change on the stage,
torrents of spring
cannot still the icy
wind from outside.

That men will speak
endlessly as of
Atreus' son
of you, too,
seems less than this breach
you struck unknowing,

struck unconscious.
Shivering,
we feel the blindness
even of princes
whose fame is so unlike
all they imagined.

Your growth is beggared
by the splintering crash.
But had you done less,
you might have fallen,
a floating leaf
that drops to sleep.

PEACE

Solid without the inner space
carved by the talons of defeat

Stúffed men who cram contracted conceits
into the distance within and smother
small blades of doubt
and the shoots of despair
with a blanket of verbiage
embroidered with smiles

Solid or stuffed
they foretaste death's peace
dreading as distant what blindly they own.

Fiery clamps pull back my flesh
emptiness presses my eyes from within
proudly I spurn the many who have
that which I long for after death.

FOLIAGE

November
like night
makes my window
a mirror.

Golden fire
burns itself out
against a dark sky
with no future
to dim its brightness.

Why fade into winter?
Why mourn the azaleas?
Masses of leaves on the ground
do not dull the flaming foliage
but make the earth glow.

Leafless
the elm imprints
grace to the last
on the iron sky.

ELM

In the left Y
of the only elm left
   will it leaf once more in the spring
   and let death wither its foliage
   or keep faith with the winter
   even when the azaleas sing?
      the full moon over a silent
      barely moving
      sea of treetops
      perfect as nudes.
         Despite the cold
         they need no green drapery.
         Like marble figures
         they are neither live nor dead.
            The elm towers above them
            a pillar supporting
            the darkening vault.
               Now the moon
               that was scarcely visible in the dusk
               rests in the right Y
               her glory enhanced
               by the spread of night.

DAVID: A CYCLE

(1943)

ABIGAIL

My beloved is a showering rain
In which I am cleansed from all iniquity;
My love is a summer storm
From which I emerge whole and strong.
I was even as a withering field,
Full of crooked blades and flowers that had not opened;
The earth was barren and knew me not,
And the sky was dry and had no pity on me.
Then came my beloved like pouring of water,
And in his embrace the flowers blossomed;
His kisses were lightning, my heart was like thunder,
Exploding the life that was in me.

A HYMN OF JOY

In the hills, by the waterfalls, I found you; your eyes were shining, and your hands were lovely: the winds and the clouds were in your embraces, and the ocean was in your kisses, writhing and vast, yet perfectly calm even in the fury of passion. The savage rivers seemed joyous, and the restless winds no longer lacking in peace.

What all the world could not give me, beloved, you are giving me now. I am growing in you beyond the confines of my body, expanding further than the sky, beyond the boundaries which were made for me. The heavens are mute and dumb, but I speak the voice of creation; the oceans are roaring with power, but I am become the lord of life. No longer need I defy the legions of nature, for even I am become legion, and the earth is mine. Hear me, all the clouds of the heavens, I am become as you so vast and so many: wait but a little while, and I shall outnumber you. I am your brother, O ocean, and your father, infinite life. I am the king of the creation, loving mountains, lakes, woods, and rivers; but my beloved I love more than the world which she gave to me, more than the flowers and more than the trees, even the hills and the waterfalls: they shall glorify her in this moment of joy and be the throne of her children for ever and ever.

A PRAYER OF DAVID

My God, that you might drown me in despair
And crush my heart upon your savage breast,
That you might bury me in your caresses
And take my life and let me be reborn!
I glory in the fire of your heart,
And when the others praise your grace and kindness,
I know you love them not and they have never tasted
Your deadly kisses which burn out the heart.

O Loving God, my blood is ever singing
And dancing in the rapture of your love.
Let others dream of distant joys and pleasures
And hope for comfort in some vast beyond.
Mine is the living God whose flaming power
Moves seas and clouds and rocks the mountains;
Mine is the God of Love to whom I sing
With every living fibre of my heart.

I have known war and exile, death and suffering,
The flames of sin which tears cannot extinguish,
I have been lonely in the midst of men
And was with you in desert mountain land;
I saw the wicked triumph and the coward laugh,
But I believe in you because their lives are poor,
And none can match the timeless joy and glory
Of those who perish in the fire of your love.

SAUL AMONG THE PROPHETS

I

He gazed upon the strangely reeling crowd
That whirled beneath him, singing, through the dust:
Their song seemed savage like the howl of beasts,
And when they fell upon the ground, exhausted,
Still trembling of the rhythm of their dance,
Their pallid faces fitfully distorted,
He thought he recognized the leering demons
Who haunted the unending desolation
Of his infernal nights. He felt so old,
And they would mock him, they would dance about him
As he had danced when he had been a boy—
And ever faster, whirling as in battle,
And blood would flow like blood that he had spilt
Until he shuddered and forbade the killing—
And Samuel appeared out of the darkness
And cheered the dancers on to kill and sing
And cursed him in the name of God—and left.

He thought he recognized their very faces,
And Samuel among them, still as stone,
With hard and burning eyes, the cruel man
Whose gory lips had never doubted God.
Why should he bear this curse and age forsaken
While others danced and blasphemed God and him:
"The Lord discarded you, we are his prophets,
We know his word, keep sulking in your tent"?

Then Saul's tremendous voice rang out above them:
"I am not yet too old to grasp you, God,
And while I live, they shall not mock you, Lord.
Look at these monsters, at this heathen breed,
Who try to capture you with pagan rites.
Ah, now I feel you as in former years,
The night is over, I am king again;
Your glory lifts me over men and mountains,
You speak to me and I proclaim your will."
And thus he stepped into their stumbling midst
With drunken majesty and pious beauty
And danced that all the prophets fled in terror—
And roared into the night and spoke to God
Until he fell, still shaking, to the ground
And lay in fever with a foaming mouth
And radiant eyes like one who in a dream
Embraces his beloved who is dead.

II

Saul's majesty lay quivering in the dust,
His royal garments torn, dirt in his hair;
And like a dog he hugged the sand,
Howling so self-forgotten through the night
That he was said throughout the land
To be the image of forsaken might.

Yet Saul dreamt of his Lord, and when he woke
That which had yesterday seemed past retrieving
Was now his own: the flux of time
Was weak against him as a broken rod,
The desert had become sublime,
And all that he beheld was full of God.

THE DEATH OF SAUL

O Lord of Passion, leave me not to age
And drown so slowly in the gloom of death!
Waves of despair are leaping at my heart:
I cannot find you; seas of sorrow flood
The ancient fields where I would graze my steers
And speak to you to ease my loneliness.
Return, my God, I am become a shadow,
Come back and be my brother as of old!

Do not despise my age—remember me!
I am so lonely for the flaming glory
Which you would pour upon me in my youth.
I shiver in the dusk and long for you,
For you created me a man of passion,
Clad me with power, crowned me with your love,
And ravaged me and left my heart a shambles
To smolder slowly to a creeping death.

I felt your presence once, you cannot leave me
Though I am helpless as a suckling babe.
Your fire is still raging in my blood,
And I remember nights of life and passion
And wars and crowns—I will not let you go,
And if you break my mind, I see you yet
And seize your glory with tremendous hands
And hold you fast and fall upon my sword.

KING DAVID'S DANCE

Blood stained the mighty rocks on which the conquered city towered, and ram horns tore the air with sounds more powerful than those which smashed the walls of Jericho. The musicians revelled in their drums, and the crowd was singing as the Ark of God entered Jerusalem. The melancholy harps alone suggested the unceasing sadness which shrouded David's life as he, the king, abandoned and inspired, danced.

There was no temple then; Michal, his wife, the daughter of the lordly Saul, despised the bold indignity of his ecstatic steps, the worthless cloth which garbed his majesty, the silent beauty of his drunken song; and Jonathan, the ever comprehending, was dead, and Absalom, his son, was yet to die. When he inherited the throne, he wept for Saul and his beloved Jonathan, although their death relieved his endless exile and made the outcast an anointed king. When he regained his crown from the rebellious armies of his son, his mourning for the prince drowned the victorious jubilation of his people. And when King David felt that he had sinned and that Bathsheba's babe had been a child of cruelty, he wept and fasted, and he wrote a song more powerful than all the kings of Asia; but when the babe died, David rose from dust and ashes, embraced Bathsheba in his deepened love, and he begat an heir, Prince Solomon, whose *Song of Songs* will live forever. But when the Ark of God entered Jerusalem, King David danced.

Speech, song, and prayers failed him in that hour. The bloodstained ruins of the conquered town reminded him that others might retake this precious prize of his so bold campaign and that his children's children might return to the unending night of bitter exile. He had survived his banishment and conquered, and yet he was an outcast even now, not only in the scorching eyes of Michal but in this singing crowd of whom he was no part. In his despair he felt the strength of those who live in beauty, he symbolized the sacred presence in this city, and made the crumbling stones of a demolished town the timeless monument of life and love and God—and danced.

DAVID AND BATHSHEBA

BATHSHEBA

Let not your love be vast like God's
In whose embrace we die like flowers in the sun.
Be not like Him who sends us floods and storms
And frightens children with His awful thunder.
I know that you are great and powerful,
Your arms are stronger than the ocean,
Your thoughts are vaster than the firmament,
Your eyes make lightning dim.
I do not know what is like you but God and nature;
You must have been before the mountains were
Which tear the clouds in heaven.

But cast aside your force and fire
And touch me gently with your hand, like this,
And stroke my hair more softly than a quiet breeze;
The feeling of your eye-lash on my forehead
Is more to me than all the furious passion
Of which I am so weary and so sad.
Be still and let the night surround us
With gracious silence and a veil of love.
Let me remember melancholy blossoms
And sleepy flowers as we had at home,
And let me dream of youth and beauty
And all the things I never had.
I feel so tired of forgetting
And burying the past in your embraces.

Ah, it was I and not some God above
Who bears the fault for all this fruitless life:
I was no different from the little flowers
Which perish in the hail in spring;
I was as empty as a radiant blossom
Which lives and dies and does not comprehend.

Beloved, all the times we spent together
Were mute and senseless like a barren desert
And fled as spring and summer pass away.
One night is left, beloved; let me be your bride:
I do not know you, let me feel your power,
Embrace me as the ocean drowns a ship,
Submerge me in the exultation of your love.

Burn me to death! One night is left
To celebrate myself, beloved:
Past, present, future mingle in a moment,
The world is fading—I feel you alone—
And floods of fire:
There are sounds of drums—
And crimson violins—
And all eternity at once.

DAVID

Sleep deeply, child, and bathe your soul in darkness
To cleanse it from the brazen insolence of time
Which is the living mirror of our crimes.
Let go yourself, abandon even love;
Descend into the valley of the shadow
Where sun and moon may never shed their light
Upon our broken lives and wasted hearts,
On ashen faces and on empty eyes.

The past is stale, tomorrow will be shallow,
But in the moment lies eternity.
Dive then beneath the realm of all existence
And lend your soul unto the night to fill it:
Let darkness pour into your heart, beloved,
And drink the purple wine of death.

Now you are lost to him:
The rising storm cannot disturb your sleep
Nor lightning raise you from the vale of darkness.
A drop of rain hangs in your hair,
Your cheeks are pale and yet alive
Like clouds reflecting still the sun that went,
And on your lips a distant smile is floating,
Elusive as a limpid butterfly.

The rain subsides, the storm has passed away.
The trees are greener now, the flowers blossom

As dawn begins to resurrect the world—
And still you smile: you think that all this beauty
Might yet restore my heart and give new life to me?

I hear the birds and see the mountains glowing,
And soon the sun will cast his light on us.
I know it well, I waited many nights
That light return and life and beauty.
But is not every day alike?
What else is nature but some vast projection
Of all the moods and feelings of my heart?
There is a sun to scorn the brilliant dreams
Which mortals ponder in their hopeful hearts,
And there is night to veil intolerable shame.
There are the mountains which are ever tempting
To higher aspirations and to bolder thoughts,
And there are rivers to suggest the endless cycles
In which my yearning soul consumes itself.

I loved the sun and prayed to lightning,
I climbed the rocks and bathed myself in snow,
Walked through the desert, lost myself in woods
And tried to drown myself within the sea.
I know that nature is the setting of a lost soul,
An opiate to get drunk on and forget
The beating of our heart when madness lurks in our eyes.

Sleep deeply, child, there is no charm in life
That sleep could not replace a thousandfold.
Sleep deeply lest the vision of a million suns
Haunt you as me: their light devours
Whatever grew on earth. All colors burn in fever—
See, my blood is boiling—red and yellow
Is all I see: there is no shadow
And no repose from life.
The drums of destiny are beating in my heart
A thundering melody of liquid fire.
I have no tears to drown them,
Death could not absolve me:
Let me live!

BATHSHEBA

The dreamless beauty of the night is fading,
The fleeting shadows of the dawn are gone,
And still the world is there.
I slumbered in the arms of life eternal,
And you were with me:
Now, why do you sit and gaze upon me
And look like petrified despair?
You did not sleep tonight, you look so sullen,
Almost dead.

Yet it was you who tore the veil of death
From my despairing eyes to show me life,
And I who walked in mortal slumber through the world
Awoke and felt that there was life within me;
My heart which had succumbed in agony
Unfolded like a tardy blossom
To drink the light and beauty of your face
And to be warm when you might touch it.

You are the lord of life and death, beloved,
And though the earth were dead and sullen,
An endless vale of sorrows, in your vision
It might gain life such as I saw this night;
For in your hands—is not the world an empty scroll
On which you write a verse and make it live?

Forget your dreams, my love,
Shake off the veil of sadness which is shrouding
Your godlike eyes and look at me.
Did you not teach me that the dreamers waste
Their lives for nothing—that they die like cows
Which stare into the distance, ever mute?

You should not brood all night and seek a purpose
For things as empty as the brilliant air:
Drink in its beauty even as I do
When I consume you with my loving eyes.
What does it matter whether there is meaning
In nature or the sullen hearts of men.
Your heart is full and overflowing
With pious beauty and the strength of love.
You have the power to bestow a meaning
On joy and pain and even death—
And those who die for you—I envy them.

You are a god, my lord,
And all the world is recreated in your stride.
The soil which you have watered with your tears,
The heavens which you comprehended in your songs,
The mountains where you suffered and despaired
Gain life from you and everlasting beauty.

You cannot die, beloved, while the world embeds
Your soul and blood and overwhelming love.
Let generations pass, whatever little meaning
Men find in life is yours, beloved, ours—
Let us go.

ABSALOM'S DEATH

When Absalom had meanly perished, King David cursed the Lord. "I envy Saul," he cried, "who died in madness; I envy Saul the very curse of God. That I had lost my life a foe of God, or that my sons had died like Jonathan! Why did He lay his evil spell on Amnon, my first-born, with his melancholy mouth, the heir of all my passion and my strength? He raped his sister, but did I not kill Uriah to possess his beauteous wife? He spent himself in one outrageous deed, while all my sins were fires which I braved to be reborn with richer heart and mind. He brooded afterwards, unable to regret and yet too weak to tell the world the beauty of his crime, and had no prayer and no verse to soothe the hostile scorn of those who knew his sin. I cannot hate my Absalom for ending Amnon's life—Amnon was dead too long before. I cannot hate my Absalom for his ambition: I coveted Saul's crown while I was singing to calm the grief which overcame his heart. I see my unrest burning in your face, but the uneven lines around your lips show how you desecrated all your graces. You courted all the small desires which are common, but the majestic longing which inspires the chosen only you have meanly drowned in banal orgies and in wanton dreams. O Lord, I need no prophets to reveal my sins: you gave me children to perpetuate my every evil thought and took them hence when they had torn my heart. My children, you have died for my transgressions, but with my life I shall atone for you."

THE LAST PSALM OF DAVID

The Lord is my lover, I am not alone:
The sky is his face and the rivers his arms;
His forehead is clouded as in deep thought,
And his hand rules the land with firmness and strength.
My age shall not frighten me, for the Lord is my lover;
Men may forsake me and women turn away,
But the Lord will look upon me and I shall know his power,
And the land shall bear fruit and be beautiful in the spring.
Golden oranges will glisten in the sun, and the cedars will
    be black,
The sheep will be like foam on a wind-stroked lake,
The shepherd's song gentle as the moon in the flood,
And the dreams of young women as a field of roses.
Keep ever forgetting me, you children of my brothers,
Never turn back to me, O women of Jerusalem;
The love of this land surpasses your graces,
And the beauty of its ripeness will outlast your ornaments.
I was old and chilly when I saw the sun,
And the flaming fruit was a promise of life.
The land is in love with me, and my Lord is the land,
God is my lover, and the earth is His beauty.
We are not of yesterday, but before you were born,
Yet I am not old, every flower is a sign of my youth,
The blossoms unfold and I see the light of the world,
When the sheep graze on the hills, I dance among them.
The land caresses me, its kisses are fragrant,
The wind strokes me and the dusk embraces me—
My beloved is with me and I shall sleep with her,
The land will hold me, and I shall not awake.

ABISHAG

Draw nearer, Abishag, the night is cold
And gloomy as the grave; the chills of death
Are hugging me and take my breath—
Draw nearer, Abishag, for I am old
And may not live to see the rising sun
Dispel the spirits which besiege my bed.
You seem so far, I live among the dead—
Come closer, Abishag, beloved one,
Embrace me, with your burning lips awaken
A spark of feeling in my freezing heart.
Be you my lyre, and the ancient art
Which soothed King Saul when God had long forsaken
His royal head shall come to me again.
I see him in the dusk, his shape is vast,
He leers at me: your turn has come at last—
And where is David now to soothe your pain?
And where is Jonathan, where Abigail,
Where Amnon, where is Absalom, my son,
Where is my glory, where my loved ones gone,
Where are my prayers? Songs and music fail,
And you, a virgin whom I do not know,
Sigh in my arms and dream of years ahead.
Come back to me, for soon I shall be dead,
My heart will stop, and you, my love, can go.

WALTER KAUFMANN was born in Freiburg, Germany. He is a graduate of Williams College. He received his doctorate from Harvard University in 1947 and in the same year joined the staff of Princeton University, where he is now Professor of Philosophy. His many books include *Critique of Religion and Philosophy, From Shakespeare to Existentialism, The Faith of a Heretic, Hegel,* and *Tragedy and Philosophy.*

Walter Kaufmann has also translated ten of Nietzsche's works, six of them available in Vintage Books along with his own book, *Nietzsche: Philosopher, Psychologist, Antichrist.* His translations of *Twenty German Poets* and *Basic Writings of Nietzsche* are available in the Modern Library.